D0630911

ISAAC ASIMOV'S NEW LIBRARY OF THE UNIVERSE

# THE BIRTH OF OUR UNIVERSE

## BY ISAAC ASIMOV

WITH REVISIONS AND UPDATING BY GREG WALZ-CHOJNACKI

Gareth Stevens Publishing
**MILWAUKEE**

**For a free color catalog describing Gareth Stevens' list of high-quality books, call 1-800-542-2595 (USA) or 1-800-461-9120 (Canada). Gareth Stevens' Fax: (414) 225-0377.**

**Library of Congress Cataloging-in-Publication Data**

Asimov, Isaac.
  The birth of our universe / by Isaac Asimov; with revisions and
updating by Greg Walz-Chojnacki.
      p. cm. — (Isaac Asimov's New library of the universe)
    Rev. ed. of: How was the universe born? 1988.
    Includes bibliographical references and index.
    ISBN 0-8368-1192-5
    1. Cosmology—Juvenile literature. [1. Universe. 2. Cosmology.]
I. Walz-Chojnacki, Greg, 1954-. II. Asimov, Isaac. How was the
universe born? III. Title. IV. Series: Asimov, Isaac. New library of
the universe.
QB983.A84  1995
523.1—dc20                                    94-31257

This edition first published in 1995 by
**Gareth Stevens Publishing**
1555 North RiverCenter Drive, Suite 201
Milwaukee, Wisconsin 53212, USA

Project editor:  Barbara J. Behm
Design adaptation:  Helene Feider
Editorial assistant:  Diane Laska
Production director:  Susan Ashley
Picture research:  Kathy Keller
Artwork commissioning:  Kathy Keller and Laurie Shock

Printed in the United States of America

1 2 3 4 5 6 7 8 9 99 98 97 96 95

To bring this classic of young people's information up to date, the editors at Gareth Stevens Publishing have selected two noted science authors, Greg Walz-Chojnacki and Francis Reddy.  Walz-Chojnacki and Reddy coauthored the recent book *Celestial Delights: The Best Astronomical Events Through 2001.*

Walz-Chojnacki is also the author of the book *Comet: The Story Behind Halley's Comet* and various articles about the space program.  He was an editor of *Odyssey*, an astronomy and space technology magazine for young people, for eleven years.

Reddy is the author of nine books, including *Halley's Comet, Children's Atlas of the Universe, Children's Atlas of Earth Through Time,* and *Children's Atlas of Native Americans,* plus numerous articles.  He was an editor of *Astronomy* magazine for several years.

# CONTENTS

We live in an enormously large place – the Universe. It's just in the last fifty-five years or so that we've found out how large it probably is. It's only natural that we would want to understand the place in which we live, so scientists have developed instruments – such as radio telescopes, satellites, probes, and many more – that have told us far more about the Universe than could possibly be imagined.

We have seen planets up close. We have learned about quasars and pulsars, black holes, and supernovas. We have gathered amazing data about how the Universe may have come into being and how it may end. Nothing could be more astonishing.

But the greatest drama of all is to try to understand the Universe as a whole. We can only begin to grasp its vastness and to study all the miraculous objects we find!

*Isaac Asimov*

## Ancient Beliefs

Long ago, humans could only wonder about the vastness of the Universe.

To ancient people, Earth seemed to be no more than a patch of flat ground that was not very big at all. The sky seemed to be a solid dome that came down to meet the ground all around, at places not far off. They thought the Sun traveled across the sky to give Earth light and warmth. The sky was blue when the Sun was present but turned black when the Sun set. In the night sky, there were many, many specks of light – or stars. The Moon, which went through changes of shape every month, moved among the stars. A few stars were brighter than the others, and they also moved.

*Top:* According to ancient Greek myths, the god Helios drove a chariot carrying the Sun across the sky.

*Bottom:* The stars of summer gleam like jewels on the dome of the night sky.

*Right:* Ancient Egyptians thought of the sky as the starry body of Nut, the goddess of the heavens.

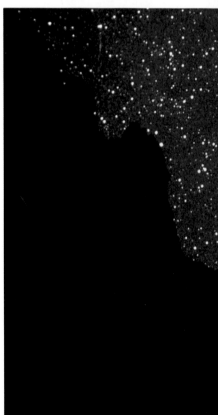

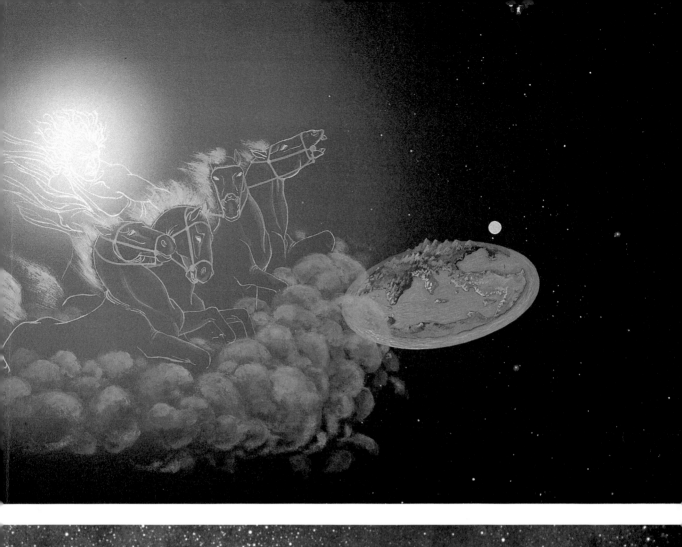

*Above:* Star trails in a time-exposure photo of the night sky. From where we stand on Earth, the Sun, Moon, planets, and stars all seem to wheel across the sky – small wonder people once thought Earth was the center of the Universe.

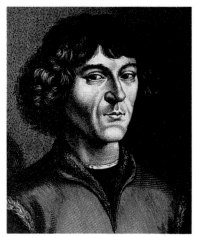

*Right:* Nicolaus Copernicus – the Polish philosopher, doctor, and astronomer who showed that the planets circle the Sun.

*Far right:* The Copernican system, with the Sun at the center of the Universe.

## The Sun Is the Center

The ancient Greeks thought Earth was a large sphere located at the center of the Universe. They thought the Moon circled Earth. Outside the Moon's orbit circled Mercury, Venus, the Sun, Mars, Jupiter, and Saturn. Outside the orbits of all these bodies were the sky and the stars.

In 1543, a Polish astronomer named Nicolaus Copernicus showed that it made more sense to think of the Sun as the center of the Universe, with the planets moving around it. He stated that since Earth is one of the planets, it also revolves around the Sun.

In 1710, English astronomer Edmund Halley discovered that the stars moved, too.

### ? Did the death of a star cause the birth of _our_ star?

The Solar System formed from a gigantic cloud of dust and gas a little less than 5 billion years ago. That cloud of dust and gas must have existed all through the life of the Universe. So the cloud was perhaps 10 to 15 billion years old when it began to collapse to form our Sun and planets. Why did the cloud collapse after all that time? Astronomers think the shock of a nearby exploding star called a supernova might have started the cloud's collapse. But they still aren't sure if that is what actually happened.

# Endless Galaxies

In 1785, English astronomer William Herschel showed that all the stars formed a large collection shaped like a lens. We call this collection the Milky Way Galaxy. This is our galaxy, and it is 100,000 light-years across. Each light-year is almost 6 trillion miles (9.5 trillion kilometers) long.

There are other galaxies as well. They look like cloudy patches in the sky. The closest large galaxy to our own is over 2 million light-years away. It is called the Andromeda Galaxy. Many other galaxies are scattered throughout space. There might be a hundred billion in all!

*Far right:* Viewed through a telescope, ragged dust clouds appear around the Andromeda Galaxy's core. Over 2 million light-years away from Earth, the Andromeda is the closest galaxy that resembles our own spiral, the Milky Way. (The white streak across the sky is the light reflected off an artificial satellite.)

*Inset:* If we could view our Milky Way from a great distance, it would look like the Andromeda Galaxy pictured here.

*Right:* Not only did William Herschel recognize our Milky Way Galaxy, he also discovered the planet Uranus and designed the best telescopes of his time.

# Galaxies' Red Shift

In 1842, physicist Christian Doppler explained why anything noisy sounds more shrill when it comes toward you, and sounds deeper when it moves away from you. A similar kind of change, or shift, happens with light.

Every star sends out light waves. The light appears bluer if the star is coming toward us, and redder if it is moving away.

In the 1920s, astronomers found that most galaxies show a "red shift." This means that they are moving away from our Galaxy. The farther away they are, the faster they move away from us. The farthest galaxies are moving away at thousands of miles (km) a second!

*Far right:* Light from a star or galaxy spreads out into a rainbow of color. Dark lines appear where the light has been absorbed by the atoms of that star or galaxy. The lines are shifted toward ever redder light as the star or galaxy moves farther away.

*Right:* Austrian physicist Christian Doppler.

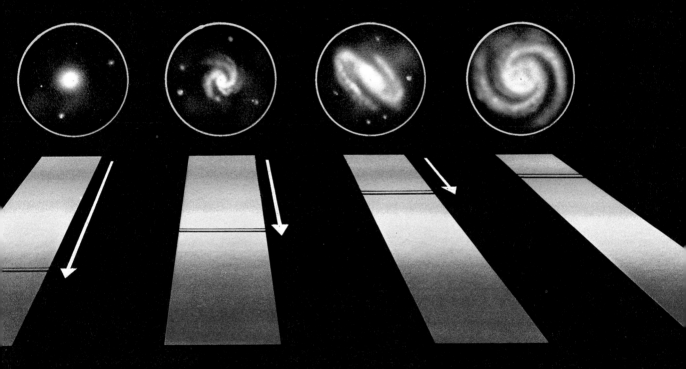

# The Big Bang

Why are all the galaxies moving away from us? What's so special about us? The answer is that *all* galaxies are moving away from each other. The Universe is always expanding, and the space between galaxies is always increasing.

Imagine time going backward. The expansion of the Universe would go backward, too – the Universe would shrink. As we go farther and farther back in time, the galaxies move closer and closer together. If we go back far enough, all the galaxies will crunch together into a small space.

That was the way it was in the beginning. Everything must have exploded in a "Big Bang." The Universe is still expanding as a result of that Big Bang. If we measure how fast the Universe is expanding, and how long it must have taken to reach its present size, we know the Big Bang happened 15 to 20 billion years ago.

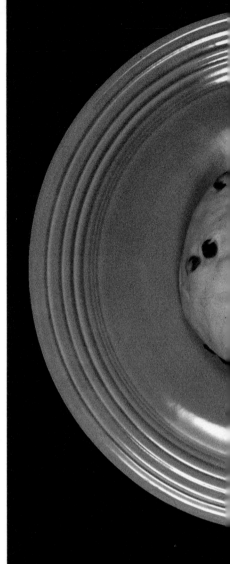

*Right.* Imagine that galaxies are like the raisins in raisin bread dough. The raisins start off fairly close together *(top)*. As the dough bakes, it expands and the raisins move away from each other *(bottom)*. As the Universe expands, the galaxies move away from each other, too.

*Inset.* A galaxy cluster. The glowing arcs in the picture might be formed by light pulled off course by a tremendous, but unidentified, source of gravity.

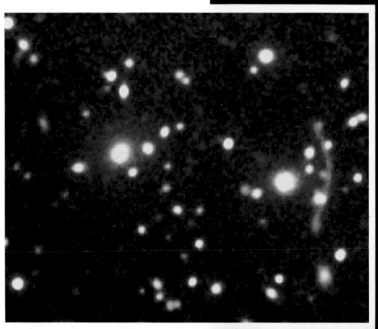

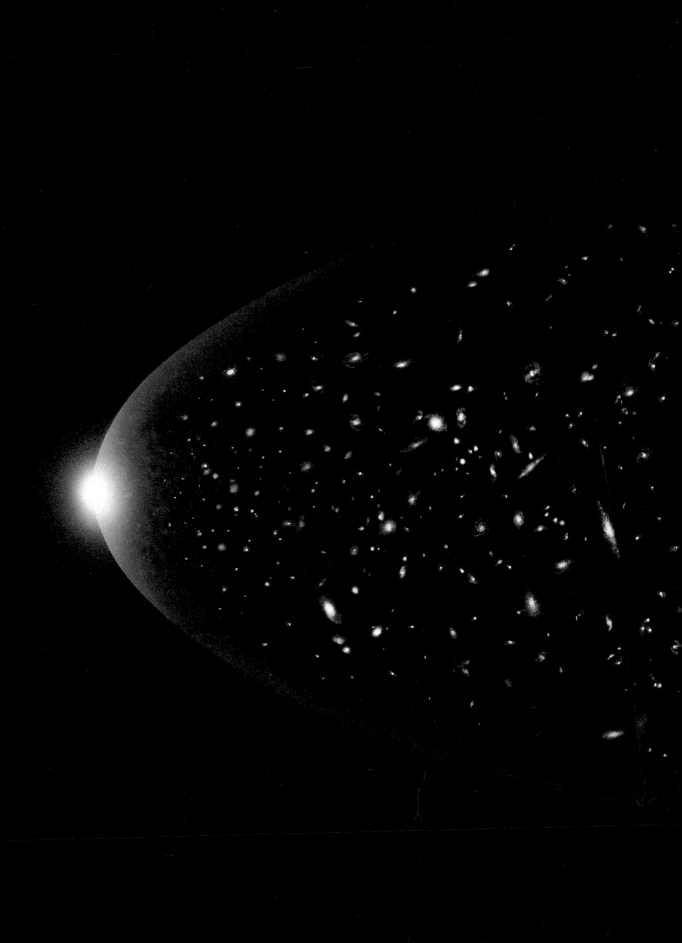

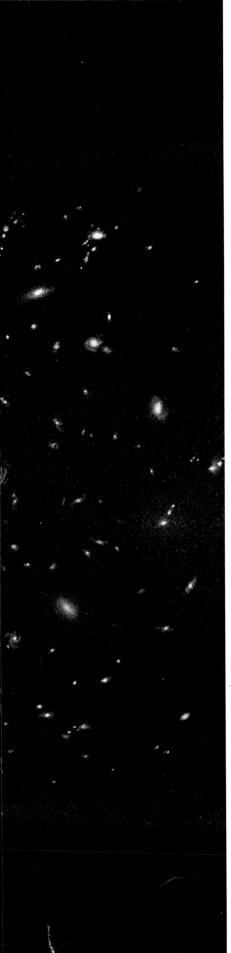

# The Big Bang's Echo

At the time just before the Big Bang when all the matter and energy of the Universe was squeezed into one tiny spot, it must have been very hot. The temperature probably registered in trillions of degrees. However, as the Universe expanded, temperatures cooled. Today, there are still hot spots, like the stars. But overall, the Universe has become much cooler over time. As the Universe cooled, the light waves of the vast flash of the Big Bang stretched and grew longer. Today, they are in the form of very long radio waves. In 1965, scientists detected these radio waves. They could hear the last faint whisper of the Big Bang of long ago.

A new spacecraft, the *Cosmic Background Explorer*, or *COBE*, was launched in 1989 to study the Big Bang's echo. *COBE* showed that the radio waves were exactly the kind predicted by the Big Bang theory.

*Left:* Our expanding Universe – the bright spot on the left represents the Big Bang. Farther to the right, subatomic particles form, then atoms of matter. Next, gas clumps together to form galaxies.

Within those galaxies, gas further clumps together to form stars and planets.

*Below:* COBE's radio map of the Universe shows radiation from the Big Bang.

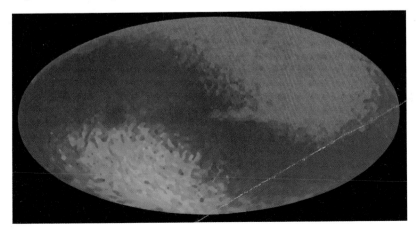

# The Universe in Infancy

Light travels at a speed of 186,000 miles (300,000 km) a second. If a star is 10 light-years from us, its light takes 10 years to reach us.

Since the Andromeda Galaxy is over 2 million light-years from us, its light takes over 2 million years to reach us. The farther out in space we look, the farther back in time we see!

Light from the most distant known quasars (very distant galaxies) takes about 12 billion or more years to reach us. Since the Big Bang happened about 15 to 20 billion years ago, we see quasars as they looked when the Universe was quite young.

In 1988, astronomers announced they had found objects in space 17 billion light-years away. These are known as primeval galaxies. We see primeval galaxies as they were in the earliest stages of their creation, before the Universe was old enough to spawn quasars. Primeval galaxies were formed when the Universe was in its infancy.

*Right:* How far is far? Light from our Sun *(upper right)* takes just 8 minutes to reach Earth *(lower left of Sun)*. Light from the nearest star after our Sun, Alpha Centauri *(the bluish speck shown below Earth)*, takes 4.2 years to reach us. Light we see from the Andromeda Galaxy *(the large spiral at lower middle)* left that galaxy over 2 million years ago. Light from the farthest known quasars *(upper left)* set out 12 billion or more years ago.

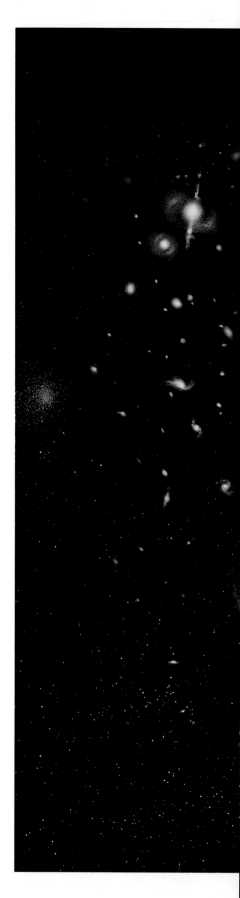

# Mapping the Universe

We might think a Big Bang would create a Universe so smooth that "lumps" of matter, such as galaxies or planets or even people, couldn't exist. But the Universe is far from smooth. In fact, astronomers have located "bubbles" of galaxies surrounding almost empty space. These lumps don't mean that the Big Bang theory is wrong. We just have a lot more to learn about the Universe.

## ? *Why is the Universe like soap bubbles?*

*Throughout the Universe, galaxies seem to form lines and even curves. If we could look at the Universe from a great distance and see it all at once, we would think it looked like soap bubbles of all sizes. The bubbles enclose large spaces in which there seems to be very little matter. Galaxies would be like the soap film making up the bubbles. The bubbles themselves would be empty.*

*Opposite:* An artist's rendition of "soap bubble" galaxies.

*Below:* The *COBE* spacecraft found tiny traces of lumpiness in the echo of the Big Bang. These are probably the "seeds" of the lumps astronomers have found in the Universe.

*Right:* Astronomers believe the Universe is shaped by matter we cannot see. This model Universe made on a supercomputer shows how invisible matter affected cosmic evolution. The "Universe cube" has 500 million light-years on each side. The "web" inside looks like the strings of galaxies actually in the cosmos.

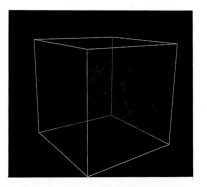

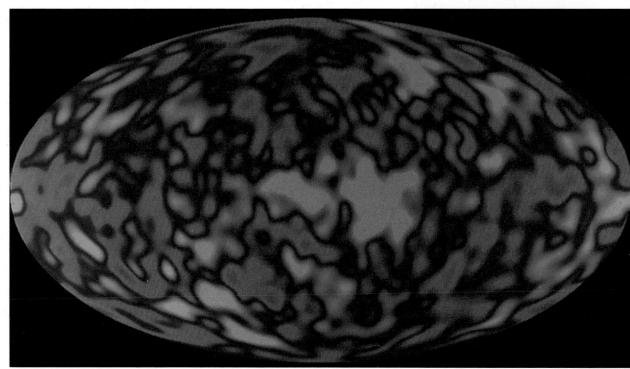

## Our Vast Universe

The known planets orbit the Sun in a region only about 7 billion miles (11 billion km) in diameter. That's just a little over a thousandth of a light-year. The nearest star after our Sun is 4.2 light-years away. That's thousands of times as far away as the farthest planet in our Solar System. The farthest stars in our Galaxy are 100,000 light-years away. The Andromeda Galaxy is over 2 million light-years away, but it's our next-door neighbor! The farthest known quasars are 12 billion or more light-years away.

In all the Universe, there are about 100 billion galaxies. And each galaxy, on average, contains about 100 billion stars. Imagine how small our own Earth is in comparison!

*Above, from left to right:*
We think of Earth as quite big, but this painting puts us in our place! As you can see, Earth is just one of nine worlds orbiting the Sun. Our Sun itself is just one of 200 billion stars in the Milky Way Galaxy. The Milky Way is but one of many galaxies in our cluster, and one of billions of galaxies in the Universe.

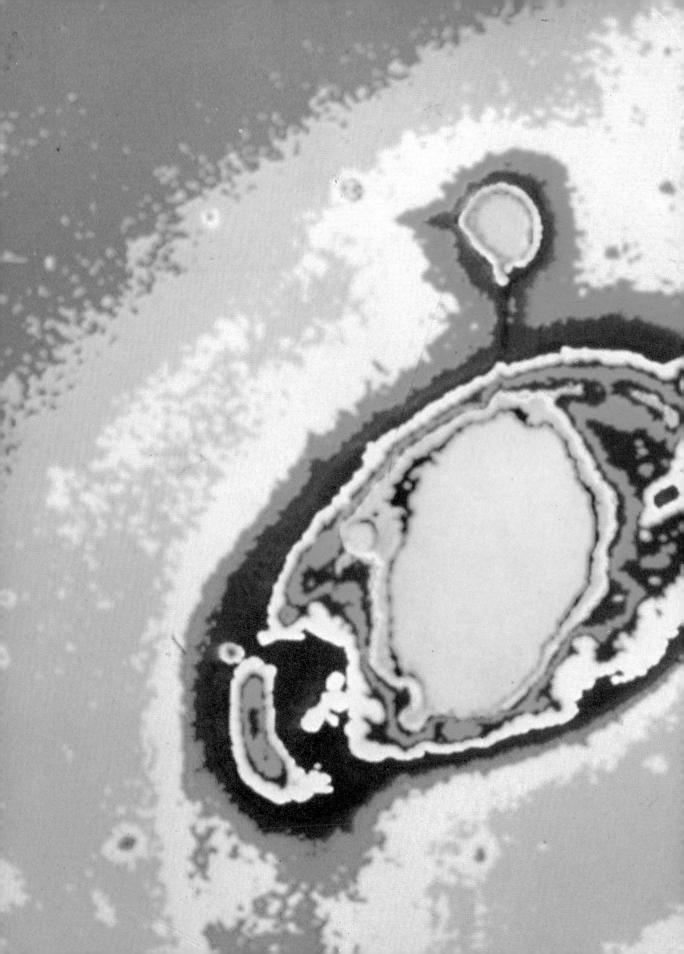

# Quasars – From a Time Before Our Sun

In the 1950s, astronomers discovered certain galaxies that sent out radio waves. They also discovered that these galaxies have the largest red shifts known. This indicates that they are an incredible distance away. Such galaxies are called quasars.

The quasars known so far are from 1 to 12 billion light-years or more away. When we look at them, we are looking back into a time before our Sun was born!

## ! *Some stars change in size!*

*Some stars pulsate, or grow larger and smaller, in a regular rhythm. They are called variable stars. The larger and brighter variable stars are, the more slowly they pulse. Therefore, scientists can tell how bright they are from how quickly or slowly they pulse. Scientists can also tell how far away the stars are from how bright they are. Scientists have studied variable stars in nearby galaxies to find out how far away the galaxies are.*

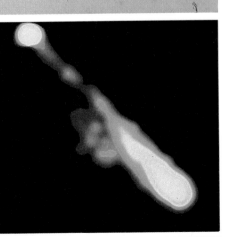

Left: Appearances can be deceiving. A bridge of gas seems to connect a quasar (top) to a galaxy (bottom). Astronomers believe that such connections are optical illusions. Colors have been added to the picture to bring out faint details.

Inset: Radio telescopes created this image of a huge gas jet erupting from quasar 3C 273. The jet is a million light-years long!

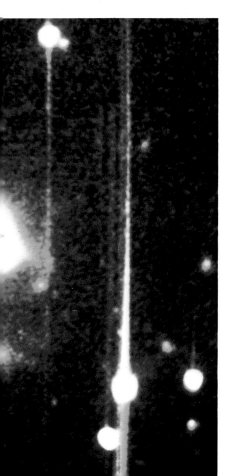

## A Supernova Beginning

Stars stay hot because of nuclear changes in their centers. As a star center grows hotter, the star expands. But eventually, the star explodes and collapses.

When a very large star explodes, it becomes what is known as a supernova. Supernovas spread their material through space. In the Big Bang, only the simplest atoms – hydrogen and helium – were formed. But supernovas spread more complex atoms outward.

Our Sun formed from a cloud with these more complex atoms. Almost all the atoms of Earth – and also in ourselves – were formed in stars that exploded as supernovas long ago.

### ! *A crab in the sky!*

*In 1054, a supernova only about five thousand light-years away appeared in the sky. It was brighter than the planet Venus. A year or so later, it faded away. What is left of it can still be seen as a small, cloudy patch in the exact place where the supernova was. It is actually a cloud of debris left by the explosion. Because of its shape, it is called the Crab Nebula. It has been expanding for almost a thousand years since the explosion. In the Crab Nebula's center is a tiny neutron star. This is all that is left of the original giant star that exploded.*

*Opposite, top:* A large star can explode with incredible violence as a supernova. A supernova releases complex elements into space, and the force of the explosion helps other stars begin to form.

*Opposite, bottom, left:* Special cameras reveal a disk of gas and dust around the star Beta Pictoris. Is this the start of another solar system?

*Above:* Galaxy NGC 5128 before *(top)* and after *(bottom)* it had a supernova *(arrow)*.

*Left:* A gas-gulping galaxy? Clouds of gas falling into a bright, young galaxy, II Zwicky 23, have caused a burst of star formation. The new stars are so brilliant that they caused streaks of light to appear on the telescope's detector.

# The Big Crunch

When a supernova explodes, what is left of it can collapse into a tiny object with gravity so strong that everything falls in, but nothing comes out. This object is called a black hole. There might be a black hole in the center of every galaxy.

The Universe may expand forever, or its own gravity might some day slow its expansion, and even stop it. It might then fall back together in a Big Crunch. And maybe a new Universe will form in a new Big Bang.

Maybe there was a Big Crunch, or even many Big Crunches, before the Big Bang that formed our Universe. Scientists do not know for certain. They are still trying to understand the Big Bang that created our present Universe. That's a big enough puzzle for now!

## Mini-stars with mega-mass

*When a star explodes and collapses, it becomes incredibly smaller than you might ever expect. It's like breaking apart a Ping-Pong ball and then packing the pieces back together in a small, tight pile. Some stars collapse into white dwarf stars. White dwarfs can be smaller than Earth, but they can hold the same amount of matter as the Sun! Still smaller stars, called neutron stars, are formed when very large stars collapse. Neutron stars can contain as much mass as our Sun, but they might be only a few miles (km) in diameter!*

Left: Someday in the very distant future, the Universe may stop expanding and begin contracting. Then everything in the cosmos would fall into an enormous black hole (top of painting). Afterward, perhaps there will be another Big Bang!

## Fact File:  Our Universe – the Enormity of It All!

We know the Universe is a big place.  But just how big is it?  Imagine that we could make the Sun the size of a soccer ball.  Then let's shrink the entire known Universe even further, so we could put the Solar System in a cup.  And finally, let's shrink the Universe down so that all of our Galaxy, the Milky Way, would be no wider than this book!

Even after reducing the Universe this much, we might be surprised at how far apart everything in the cosmos still seems.  Use the illustrations (above and opposite) and the information (opposite) to get an idea of how big and how far away everything in the Universe is.  As big as we think Earth is, it is only a tiny speck in our vast Universe!

## The Sun as a Soccer Ball

- What if the Sun were...a soccer ball about 8 3/4 inches (22 centimeters) wide?

- Then Earth would be...a pebble less than 1/10 inch (1/4 cm) wide, and about 78 3/4 feet (24 meters) from our soccer-ball Sun.

- And Jupiter (the Solar System's biggest planet) would be...a bit bigger than a small ball bearing that is 7/8 inch (2.2 cm) wide.

- And Pluto (our Solar System's tiniest known planet) could be...a pebble smaller even than Earth, about 1/2 mile (0.8 km) from our soccer-ball Sun.

- And Alpha Centauri (the nearest star in our Galaxy, besides our Sun) would be...almost 4 miles (6.4 km) from the soccer-ball Sun at the center of our Solar System.

## The Milky Way as a Book

- And what if the Milky Way (our Galaxy) was... a book almost 1 foot (30 cm) wide?

- Then the Andromeda Galaxy (the galaxy "next door") would be...about 23 feet (7 m) away from the Milky Way.

- And the farthest-known quasars would be...about 32 miles (51 km) away from the Milky Way!

## The Solar System in a Cup

- And what if our Solar System were... small enough to fit in a cup?

- Then the Milky Way (our Galaxy) would be... as wide as North America – about 3,000 miles (4,800 km) across!

# More Books about the Universe

*Mysteries of Deep Space: Black Holes, Pulsars, and Quasars.*  Asimov (Gareth Stevens)
*Nightwatch: An Equinox Guide to Viewing the Universe.*  Dickinson (Camden)
*Our Vast Home: The Milky Way and Other Galaxies.*  Asimov (Gareth Stevens)
*Space and Beyond.*  Montgomery (Bantam)
*The Stars: From Birth to Black Hole.*  Darling (Dillon)
*Universe.*  Zim (Morrow)
*Universe: Past, Present and Future.*  Darling (Dillon)

# Videos

*How Was the Universe Born?*  (Gareth Stevens)
*Our Solar System.*  (Gareth Stevens)

# Places to Visit

You can explore many places in the Universe without leaving Earth.  Here are some museums and centers where you can find a variety of space exhibits.

The Space and Rocket Center
  and Space Camp
One Tranquility Base
Huntsville, AL  35807

Astrocentre
Royal Ontario Museum
100 Queen's Park
Toronto, Ontario  M5S 2C6

Seneca College Planetarium
1750 Finch Avenue East
North York, Ontario  M2J 2X5

San Diego Aero-Space Museum
2001 Pan American Plaza
Balboa Park
San Diego, CA  92101

National Air and Space Museum
Smithsonian Institution
Seventh and Independence Avenue SW
Washington, D.C.  20560

Anglo-Australian Observatory
Private Bag
Coonarbariban 2357  Australia

# Places to Write

Here are some places you can write for more information about the Universe.  Be sure to state what kind of information you would like.  Include your full name and address so they can write back to you.

NASA Lewis Research Center
Educational Services Office
21000 Brookpark Road
Cleveland, OH  44135

Sydney Observatory
P. O. Box K346
Haymarket 2000  Australia

Canadian Space Agency
Communications Department
6767 Route de L'Aeroport
Saint Hubert, Quebec  J3Y 8Y9

National Space Society
922 Pennsylvania Avenue SE
Washington, D.C.  20003

# Glossary

**Andromeda Galaxy:** the closest galaxy to our own Milky Way Galaxy, although it is over two million light-years away.

**atoms:** the smallest particles of elements that can exist. Atoms are the source of nuclear energy when joined together or split apart.

**the Big Bang:** a gigantic explosion that some scientists believe created our Universe.

**billion:** the number represented by 1 followed by nine zeroes – 1,000,000,000. In some countries, this number is called "a thousand million." In these countries, one billion would then be represented by 1 followed by twelve zeroes – 1,000,000,000,000 – a million million.

**black hole:** an object in space caused by the explosion and collapse of a star. This object is so tightly packed that not even light can escape the force of its gravity.

**galaxy:** any of the billions of large groupings of stars, gas, and dust that exist in the Universe. Our galaxy is known as the Milky Way Galaxy.

**light-year:** the distance that light travels in one year – nearly 6 trillion miles (9.5 trillion km).

**nebula:** a cloud of dust and gas in space. Some large nebulas, or nebulae, are the birthplaces of stars. Other nebulae are the debris of dying stars.

**neutron stars:** very small stars that form when large stars collapse. Much of the very great mass of the large star is kept in the neutron star.

**quasars:** distant galaxies in the Universe. They are billions of light-years away from Earth.

**radio waves:** electromagnetic waves that can be detected by radio-receiving equipment.

**red shift:** the apparent reddening of light given off by an object moving away from us. The greater the red shift of light from a distant galaxy, the farther that galaxy is moving away from us.

**sphere:** a globelike body. The ancient Greeks felt Earth was a large sphere at the center of the Universe.

**supernova:** the result of a huge star exploding. When a supernova occurs, material from the star is spread through space.

**Universe:** everything that we know exists and believe may exist.

**variable stars:** stars whose brightness changes. Some variable stars change brightness regularly. Others are unpredictable.

# Index

Born in 1920, Isaac Asimov came to the United States as a young boy from his native Russia. As a young man, he was a student of biochemistry. In time, he became one of the most productive writers the world has ever known. His books cover a spectrum of topics, including science, history, language theory, fantasy, and science fiction. His brilliant imagination gained him the respect and admiration of adults and children alike. Sadly, Isaac Asimov died shortly after the publication of the first edition of *Isaac Asimov's Library of the Universe*.

The publishers wish to thank the following for permission to reproduce copyright material: front cover, © Julian Baum 1988; 4, Courtesy of Julian Baum; 4-5 (upper), © Sally Bensusen 1988; 4-5 (lower), © Frank Zullo 1987; 6, AIP Niels Bohr Library; 6-7 (upper), © Anglo-Australian Telescope Board, David Malin; 6-7 (lower), Mary Evans Picture Library; 8, Courtesy of Julian Baum; 8-9 (large), National Optical Astronomy Observatories; 8-9 (inset), © George East 1978; 10, Courtesy of Julian Baum; 10-11, © Brian Sullivan 1988; 12, National Optical Astronomy Observatories; 12-13, © Julian Baum 1988; 14-15, © Paternostro/Schaller 1988; 15, NASA; 16-17, © Paternostro/Schaller 1988; 18 (upper), Courtesy of Michael Norman, University of Illinois; 18 (lower), NASA; 19, © Julian Baum 1988; 20-21, © Brian Sullivan 1988; 22-23, National Optical Astronomy Observatories; 23, Science Photo Library; 24 (upper), © Mark Paternostro 1988; 24 (lower), Jet Propulsion Laboratory; 24-25, 25 (both), National Optical Astronomy Observatories; 26-27, © Mark Paternostro 1988; 28-29, © Larry Ortiz 1988.